Nourishment
Anne Le Marquand Hartigan

salmonpoetry

Published in 2005 by
Salmon Publishing,
Cliffs of Moher, County Clare, Ireland
Website: www.salmonpoetry.com
email: info@salmonpoetry.com

Copyright © Anne Le Marquand Hartigan, 2005

ISBN 1 903392 48 9

All rights reserved. No part of this publication may be reproduced or transmitted in any form or by any means, electronic or mechanical, including photography, recording, or any information storage or retrieval system, without permission in writing from the publisher. The book is sold subject to the condition that it shall not, by way of trade or otherwise, be lent, resold or otherwise circulated without the publisher's prior consent in any form of binding or cover other than that in which it is published and without a similar condition, including this condition, being imposed on the subsequent purchaser.

Cover artwork: 'In the Wake of The Moon' by Anne Le Marquand Hartigan
Cover Design & Typesetting: Siobhán Hutson
Printed by Alma Pluss SIA, Riga, Latvia

*"Even though Shakespeare said everything,
Horace is more to me, he mysteriously perceived
the sweetness of being…"*
AKHMATOVA

Acknowledgments

"Epistles In Winter" was first published in *The White Page/An Bhiléog Bhán: Twentieth-Century Irish Women Poets*, edited by Joan McBreen, Salmon Publishing, 1999.

"Epistles in Winter" and "The Hearth Stone" appeared in *Podium 4*, edited by Noel King, Samhlaiocht Chiarrai, published by Kerry Arts.

"The Hawser", published in *The Clifden Anthology*, edited by Brendan Flynn. Clifden Community Arts Week. 2002

"The White Cloth" published in *Poetry NZ* August 2003 and read by Anne Le Marquand Hartigan at Dublin Writer's Festival 2003.

"Care, A Charm" is performed by Anne Hartigan in the forthcoming film *God, Smell and Her* by Karin Westerlund to be premiered in Stockholm in September 2005

Contents

Pressed Down and Running Over	9
A Plain Chant	10
Grounded	11
Sweet Tooth	12
Throw	13
The Stream	14
The Hearth Stone	15
Under All Unions	16
Nourishment	17
Epistles in Winter	18
Elysium	20
Possession	22
Reel	23
Wing	24
The Act	25
The Gatepost	26
Hills of Kerry	27
Without Hindrance	28
This Journey	29
Fire and Moon	30
The Window Eye	31
As Trees Heavy With Blossom	32
Aubade	33
Care, A Charm	34
The Wildness of Storm	36
A Sweep of Mists	37

Ill Wind	38
The White Cloth	39
Solace	40
Union	42
Lyracrompane	43
A Fragment	45
Unsweet Dreams	46
A Tint of Madder	49
Vacant Possession	50
Sunflower	51
The Cool Mouth	52
Food for the Imagination	53
Into Fresh Air	54
Taking Time Apart	55
Charting the Waters	58
The Suitcase	59
The Weather Channel	60
The Hawks Taking Unto Themselves	61
Fodder	62
The Power of The Immaterial	63
Fat Cat	64
Speaking To No One At All	65
The Hawser	66
What's The Point of It?	67
Requiem For a Brother	68
The Kind Provider	70

Pressed Down and Running Over

Here, take this

scatter of poems before you
an attempt at   country,   the need
of grassbank,   branch and silence,

always meeting in cities
a shroud of car-roar   this
is a frail attempt at petals,

libations to the Gods, those fellows –
who approve waste in their worship,
flowers, wine, candles, incense. Body.

The full abandon.

A Plain Chant

You and I steal heaven
Ah No! We make it —
didn't I spread the blue sheet
of infinity under you? Make stars?

You carried nectar under your arm —
under your tongue — we make ritual —
a rhythm that encompasses rise and fall.
A plain chant. A full cup. Splash libations

This is expanse — however small the time
All heals in the gift of tongues.

Grounded

When you came like earth
I lay down to rest.

Earth that grows words
that release burdens

slavery of mind
to the yellow balloon of the sun.

Earth holds
growth of grass.
You are green,

Your words fondle
earth tilth. Heat.
The pulse, the seed, the flower.

Sweet Tooth

The stolen fruit hardly picked
hardly in the hand
hardly the first bite taken –

the sweet juice,
the sweet word,

the long silence.

Throw

I have pitched
My bread upon your waters

Eat me slowly
Dissolve me sweetly

Taste me
Taste me

My tender flesh
My flowing wine

The Stream

I would lead my words to flow for you
sweetly I would have them run

with touch light as fingers on you
harmony and music in them
steps in them, jokes and jingles for you
full words, laughter with you
as wine deep warm, as wine crisp,
flight and winged – word power pulse pound
taunt and tightening fierce
words careful word time taking tender
take time, tangled careless care
free caught and catching,

as if we were together, in silence   still,
maybe a stream streaming   and we undressing

The Hearth Stone

"The year and the hour that snatch our day warns us not to hope for eternal life" — Horace Odes Book 1

It is on our private altars that we dare
build celebratory fires.

We have lit them in the face of obstacles,
we know danger but step on the burning coals,
because in those flaming depths
breath lives — fire of youth fire of life —
without or denied this life, the tongue dries.

We take it naked and alone and make
no apology to the Gods or the world.

This feast is a kind of fast,
waiting for time to drop, where
birth and death
happen in the one instant.

Under All Unions

Our divide bears fresh fruit,
ancient orders of birth, difference,
Old bone. Vital spit. Blood. Rapturous skin,
all this separateness — this other.

Under all unions the breach stutters,
knowledge of fire, the impossible eager knowing —
then the lack. Silence. Commitments. Trysts.
Family imprints tug like death, spurn like birth, block

with imprimaturs of light and dark.
The bell and the tolling clock. Timer and screech.
Huge pasts we peel off to slither
through those iron gates

into the slanted light of a flecked garden.
Honest body, kind eye, simple adultery.
Fingers, waters, the list to sweetness.
Of flesh. Holy sin — it is only giving.

Nourishment

Because I have lain on your deep Africa
Gorse light and dusty cinnamon, burnt umbers
You drank deep of my waters north and south,
Arising dripping, a dark god. Knowledge of interiors.
How simple to exchange continents, to play so easily
A classic music.

Child's play, intricate and private, allowing love space
To move in. A sacred grove, rowan, ash, laurel
To cast and shed spells. This enchantment is as natural
As the moon. This is the first touch. Shock: your unknown
Face, skin. I roam in ochres, duns, siennas, gifts
Spread before me on the white cloth. This is the necessary
Air and water, the bread my mouth waters for, it can go on.

Epistles in Winter

Estuary

Through you I touch many continents
many childhoods
times past of blood and love, cold
countries thaw
and the hot do not burn up, but
warm on

We make children in the night with
no darkness
in our mingling spittle words brood
the lip-lap
of language makes channels for flow
for gush
for the swift mind – the touch imperative.
We're cousins of bone and steel,
yet we melt

Saline

clash of brine and flesh
bog-wine
dung song peat tone, ice of salt
cracks a note. Staccato of teeth and bite.
The edge of black/white. Tongue of difference
spear bud – acid spring ache
the lick of it. Hard spit.

River

Bend your head and I will baptise you
so you can surface into the watermoon
there are prayers arrayed, chants and candles
melodies of blessings sing in the bird's throat
supplications of incense call our introits
they spiral into the ether breath
the moon catches and the sun consumes

eat my body.

Bend your head and with oil I will anoint you,
genuflect, kneel together in this solemn novena
take nine first Fridays to ensure a pathway
standing as the Baptist up to his knees in the flow
holding a shell to plunge, dip the waters.
The thirst drove us here, total immersion, risking
belief without doubting where enchantment burns,

drink my blood.

Elysium

I have been to Elysium.

There are no maps to find it.
Or marks on trees.

Nothing easy or difficult
Along the way to show you,

You cannot plan or strain
Put away all ideas of an
Organised expedition.

It is no good squeezing the eyesight
To try and see in the distance.

Love is dangerous.
Danger on its every needle.

Calculations and ideas are out of order,
Nothing wild or heroic nor fine-minded, No

Revolutions with bristling pistols
No overturning tables, this,

Is all slow motion.

But now the revolving round
Moon and Sun and through them

Swinging on lazy swings
Of snow and firelight,

Down long low loops
Words and whispers

An O of music
For us to rest in.

A new song,
Born from the dark.

Possession

I hold you in the crook of my arm
I hold you in the sweat of my fist
I balance you on the thin skin
on the back of my hand

I draw you in on my breath

Reel

If you lived with me
it would be light and sweet

child's play

if you lived with me
who'd know night and day

we'd meet

and laugh and be
remembering life is short

and steep
and slips away.

Come let's take it

quick

before it fades
before we fade

Wing

We live in peril
and on it,
it is our bird,
it wings us

our fragility
swept up
against the clouds.

Air takes us
we give it our bird cage bones

The roll-line of hills.
Stars were there.
The bark of dogs.

Dark night is there.
We cannot rest in it.

The Act

I will not bed with you
  until I spend days with you
    days and nights with you
      time with you
        each minute with you
          the sweat drying on us
            as if in the act of birth
              until our bodies fall apart
                killing ourselves in the act of love

The Gatepost

We talk in secrets.
It is so quiet
without your breath.

Look into the still night
we lie like stars in the arms of
the dark.

Outside the frost-fox bites
teeth ivory with death.

All creatures have their place.
Know it. They live, they die.

You wait by the gatepost.
Naked.
I enter into your dream.

Hills of Kerry

lie down low in the night air.
How are the stars?

Your swift sweep across the sky
clouds swing over you.

O lie low down
on a couch of sure clover

cold, wet,
but, yet, one step

our life
our death.

The earth's body
rests safely
under grey clouds

your body
lies safely
in mine

but then,
the rain
comes.

Without Hindrance

When I take my clothes off
  to be with you
    it is the bare fact
      of myself. My simple
        body faults
          weaknesses failures
            scars lie there. It
              is how I am now.
                Nakedness is
                  what it says. I judge myself
                    removing my cheerful disguises.

            Touching skin takes me straight
            to the heart. The feeling bit.
          The place I want to give you.
          The place I want to draw you to.

This Journey

I don't know were your heart lies.
Do you put it down?
Where rests it?

Who is its guardian?
What walks does it take and
are they long?

The paths are everywhere.
Which one does your heart travel?
What games does it play?

How sings its song?

There is an empty sound,
the sound of ice, even
if there are roars of fires.

The snow splatters on the
warm black.
Give me your arms,

in winter we must crawl
into sweetness,
blankets and down.

Come sweet snow
quieten our lives.
Damp down cool brows.
Transform and touch each
brief leaf. Tame black.

Fire and Moon

a Waltz

I cannot make a song for us
it must be silence
I cannot call out your name
yet you are not nameless

Moon knows about it.
She never blabs.
She's old old old – and tired.
She shrinks, then grows again.

She does it on purpose.
She keeps control of her heart
shrivelling it when there's
fire danger.

Fire danger lies there.
I will not let it eat me.
I have been devoured before
by the puny beast.

So when your burning comes
I fade, as a small moon, I fade.
Lying on the night's back
curled in a night's arms.

The Window Eye

If you were a real wanderer,   you would return
on horse back   mule back   or with many packhorses
snorting and smelling   stamping   all
arrival   clatter and din   commotion

or sleek in the night   a whisper   a shiver
of sheet   fingers   from your bosom   your breast
or a chest opening   flowing   silk and aromas
scents of Araby   a flood of finery   a waste of luxury
fullness   the overflowing

how our burdens ease with arrivals –
how I close the window on departure.

As Trees Heavy With Blossom

There is nowhere else to go
it is the inevitable journey
it is deeper than deepness.

It is your own dark
you own it entirely
I lie down in it.

You say:
You are safe with me

For the first time
in centuries, I am safe,

You say:
This is adoration of life,

You say:
There is love here

We bow down together
As heavy trees we bow down.

Aubade

Lie along your body
   lie down   all the way
      stretch   not to know   let
         the world flow   overhead
            high stars crackle in flight
               they are not for us let them be

                   we have drawn the night   over us
                 rest your warm wing
                     skin lies quiet on skin   cheat
                        eternity, there is only   our breath
                      our heart thump
                          the beat   the living beat

Care

A Charm

This my prayer:

This my prayer for you
This light day for you
                              Pray for you
God's hand for you
                            Stand for you

The green land for you
The wet grass for you
Swallow's wing for you
The sea's sand for you
The rock's strength for you
The tree's song for you
Thistledown for you

Silence for you
Cloud for you
Rain for you
No pain for you
No hurt befall you
A kind step for you
A soft word for you
What I have kept for you
In my heart for you
I will not part for you
treasure kept for you
Warm for you
Away from storm for you

No alarm for you
Keep all harm from you
For this night for you
Dream of light for you

This my charm for you

For this day for you
This I pray for you

This my prayer.

The Wildness of Storm

The wind is howling
its   force   its passion

this wind wants the roof
top –   off off.
Nothing else matters

except I lie with you
close as earth with rain.

A Sweep of Mists

Now the sweet rain
keeps all this safe,

the damp grasses
drip,   balance,
berries of crystal,

we catch each other's kisses
and dissolve,   and become,
in the sweep of mists,

in the drop.

Ill Wind

We creep towards the centre of winter
       down days, down, down
down – crawling away from the sun.

Where are you, Sun and Love ? Forgotten
       or impossible – those kisses sweet
as warm strawberries, memories of lips

dreams they are –   ripe for picking
       melt in the fingers   left – with a dribble
a stain –   O love   I do believe in you !

Waiting – I hope – behind glum clouds. Yes
       I believe in you; in your eye,
in the thud, thud, thud, of your pulse.

The White Cloth

If you were coming –
  I would iron the white cloth –
    Spread it on the table –
      Get out my best glasses –
        Crystal   oh sparkle –

The wine I would take
  Cool from the freezer
    Laid there to cool quickly – Out
      Before it could
        Burst –

I would walk up and down
  Look in the mirror –
    My hand shaking – applying
      My lipstick – eye shadow blurring
        Who's that in the mirror?

But when you have come
  What use would it be ?
    You undoing the buttons of my blouse
      I undoing the buttons of your shirt
        Straight to the sheet of the bed we would be –

Table
  Left to itself.
    Glasses – cold – still
      On the table.
        The white cloth
          Spread

Solace

When I think of my treasure
my heart turns sideways

                        my white bird
                my raven
                    my brown earth

                              leaves green

green green they are,   but
no hiding in them,   no safety,

sideways the glance
from his eyes,

                  so swift
                        my fire
                  my warmth

what blanket can we
        rest under?

These winds have
knife in them

edges of hills
grind their teeth.

          my laughter
             my fun
        neat,   clean,

  a deer stepping
          a wild hare
              jinxing,

            here,

wind eats all
sheering hill to bone,

lonesome we are,
far,

far far from all
that brings

            solace

Union

this wish – this draw
   this lean – this movement –
      this stillness, this wait – this
knowledge – this ignorance –
   this pull – this earth – this mud –
      this nothing at all. This barrier
this being – this dark – this
  warm – this quiet – this untalkable –
      this in explainable.   This torture –
this peace.   This farce – this funny –
   this light – this time – this O

Lyracrompane

Sweetness in the Name

The body of the hill
folds over, holds out
hands to the rain

Lyracrompane
Lyracrompane
Lyracrompane

is a love call to the earth itself.

The ground holds
the cries of the past

Lyracrompane

deep cries just under
the soil's crust

Lyracrompane

all the time the earth
is purifying crimes

turns them slowly
into growth

Lyracrompane

the name carrying a benediction –
the energy of a kiss.

Lyracrompane

              Abbydorney
Abbyfeal *Knocknagashel*
Duagh   *Castleisland*
Lixnaw   *Templeglantine*
Fingue   *Tralee*

              Lyracrompane

A Fragment

You're mostly careless
    with my love

throw it down in grass
    to lie

although it fits you
    like a glove

soft like feathers
    of a dove

it only is a little
    thing

let it shrivel wrinkle
    sigh

glimmering in the
    summer light

glimmering in the
    grass to die.

Unsweet Dreams

Because of coffee
taken late
    I meet the morning
    early –

I lie here
with out a mate
    straight haired
    or curly –

Is this how we
meet our fate
    out of step
    and churley

catch a breath
in such a state

toss and turn
ourselves berate
    in a sweat
    and surly

with life or death
we have a date
    never falling
    fairly

t'is sleep I want
at any rate
    landing on me
    squarely

dreams to come
and tuck me up
    call me sweet
    and dearie

but night, it just
hammers on
    the moon slides by
    so pearly –

full and round
complete it is,
    staring at me
    surely

Underneath its
chilling beams
songs of love
are out of date
    my mind goes round
    so whirly

if I sleep now
I'll wake up late

oh I am in a
shocking state

perhaps I'd better
masturbate

forget about the
heaven's gate?

O Morning will you
never come
and send the sun
    to shine upon
    this girly

who's lost all hope
does toss and curse
this night has been
the blasted worst

and as I reach the
final verse I've bills
to pay, my zip has burst
I've put on weight,
that's not the worst
Oh where is love,
give me a break
pale morning creep
its place to take,
in shattered sleep
a head that aches
this life is all a
bloody fake and just
you note the big mistake
to live a life
let them eat cake, just

because of coffee
taken late
    to greet this morning
    early.

A Tint of Madder

You talk of Rose Madder,
You talk of love.
Madder and madder;
And the rose.

Fugitive.
Who is running running,
Do we run from love
To become madder and madder?

The Rose is fugitive.
Opens wide, dying in its love cry
To the sun and bee.

So we will talk of the fugitive
Rose. Not love.

No no, we will not
Talk of love.

Or dye like the fugitive Rose.

I will paint your spectacles
Rose Madder with love.

NOTE: Rose Madder is an oil paint;
a semi-permanent, fugitive colour.

Vacant Possession

There is no Chair.
No place at the Table.

No Cup my lips
have drunk from.

No Dregs. Look
how clean your Sheets are

Quite clear and empty
of my Smell.

The Air has not parted for my
Body to enter. The Door is quite

innocent and vacant.
When it swings shut

I am not a memory
on the Doorstep.

The Sound
of its clunk does not

know me. The Lock
in whose Keys

press in, press in
and their Turn

is a time
without my knowledge.

Sunflower

I don't want to wait for the end
I don't want that blank — that this pen
would no longer describe a journey

knocking on doors and shouting through letterboxes,
all the invisible games the yes's and no's the words
and talk — lying together, both noisy and silent

I won't take on that huge and inevitable silence
that end would bring.

I would have to have another growing sunflower
its face following me around and around
with smiles — to shadow and clean the darkness
from the lack of your sound.

The Cool Mouth

You find me already in the bed
your outdoor kisses
your body fully clothed

And so you feel the inside
with your cool out. Sweetheart,
that's what's it's about.

Food For The Imagination

In my house walks
an imaginary cat

she twiddles between
space and hope

her soft paws
pad no imprint

she does not know
days or years   her

purrs rumble the air
her calm eyes blink

love. Yes   love.
Don't be so surprised –

with her tail she can say anything –
correct me with the flat-back

of her ears. I can feel
her body sweep my legs and

as I go upstairs   she pat-pats
my calf   reminding me

that even she,
as all imaginations do,

need food.

Into Fresh Air

Thinking of us; younger
fast footed on the move
the move forward   into new air
taking bounds for adventure
shifting   impossible stones. Taking on all
that came with love's responsibility.

The dash and dance of
physical movement
entrancing daylight and dark –
the night and day of it.
Word and brush – colour and line –
marking. Marking time.

Taking Time Apart

caught me
                in the stream

still flowing
                on the motion

flesh still
                in the fall

body
                still lost

still sailing

                slowly down

a leaf
        zig zagging

across
                air

        still feather
        still boat
          upping
            and downing
                tipping over

on the wave and
                inside   so
inside
        self
so in

                and out and found   so
moving
            back into a normal
un-real
        a whip cracking
self
    into a space

am no longer fitted for

        a space

unreal as
            normal time

2

You did not tell me the number of minutes
exactly. You did not measure it out
from a jug. Saying – Here you are,
drink this – This is quite full and complete
but it will only last for this – day.

You didn't tell me the long of it.

So when these minutes stopped I was
shut down. Stopped with the door of time
in my face. My face had left its features
on the pillow. And my blood was all drained
into the wastepaper basket.

The bones went on by themselves, sort of OK.
You know what bones are. Brittle. My self
went off on its own – tying up shoelaces

so the feet could walk, very cleverly and
take control. Moving somewhere
from there to here wherever that is
if you know those places inside.

3

Peeled back to the very
core – where the pips lie
in the centre. They are all gone.
Given away on the sea of birth.
What lies there now is the original
centre where all began.

The child lies there without defence
once the centre is entered. Hidden things
invisible to the naked mind only felt
in touches. Down in this dangerous area
the fire glows – it never goes out.

It might defeat death.
And it might not.

I opened that core yesterday
knowingly moved in again, risking life –
giving me life too. I am recovering
like a bad patient – tossing in the bed –
holding back tears like a teenager.

Charting the Waters

I can throw myself on your rock,
allow all edges to dissolve, this is trust.

I can open up into depths,
plunge into fathoms unexplored,
interiors not opened, silences and music.

I can dare this because you stand
fully accepting as if I might be
the treasure you desire.

Together we enter a world only made
with our meeting. Outside time,
life, all the practical –

on the sheet's white, we become,
give birth, double life dizzily, the cup
overflows – spilling.   Don't mention

the word love.
It is a feather floating lip lop lopsidedly
crazily into the dream

The Suitcase

I have a vision
of unhappiness
and me pushing this

behind

and saying
I want air, life, taste, fun
and running.

I make it to the station.
Why are there those
black suitcases, waiting?

The Weather Channel, Florida 2001

Lying in a world of sun and water
couples create their twosomes,
pairs lie out in chairs, recline
toward the soil and spread their
bones under the sun's bald stare.

Just lie there. Far from homes,
responsibilities locked away,
they make dull hay, letting the mind
give in to the sun's bind. Starved
of heat, they lose the grip of grey,
the bright morning's release and
allow the play of sweeter things.

Careful couples who move together
into this, still carry between them
their own personal weather.

The Hawks Taking unto Themselves
Florida 2001

Over this flimsy city, the huge wings circle,
circle, circle upward, their tilt and sweep enormous,
overshadowing air. They lean on untouched space,
their supreme wings utterly over us. Unperturbed
by roar and tarmac, they sail the thermals, rule with great flight.

Down on our concrete,
we shrivel in formal space,
civilized and timorous under
their fierce and final grace.

Fodder

You are like a big feast
that I eat slowly,
in little bits, sips
savoured. Not
munched up, not
gobbled.

You are riches
matured, spicy,
fragrant, smooth
as old whiskey.

You fill up all things
yet take no space –
simple as air
I can be drunk on you
a tipsy angel.

The Power of the Immaterial

At odd moments
I remember I love you.

It is not need
that makes love.

Love lies outside of things,
days, work accomplished,
in some ways, is immaterial.

I don't want to be missing you
or you to miss me.

I like to think of you totally
absorbed in work
just as I am, now
at this diligent moment.

So when we speak on the phone
or when we meet to unpeel
we both are present – absolutely.
Laughter mingling with the juice of mouths.
Full in the moment. There.

Fat Cat

I place my care for you
a saucer of milk on the carpet
so you can lick me up
with your pink tongue

tip tip, flick flick, flicking my
tight surface of pale cream
leaving perfect
the swiftly sinking O

dissolving into china
dissolving into you, fat cat
as you smile, sweeping drips
of pale moisture from your

furred and generous jaws.

Speaking to No one At All

You have absolutely no idea
how my blood aches in my veins
because you are far from me.

How I built a citadel
and now its crashed.

The burnt out shell is there.
Is that me I see walking over the river,
charred, burnt, a cinder walking

telling tales,
without a tongue.

The Hawser

Throwing a Line

In the deep pause of night
I can think of you
heavy limbed and lying

turn to me across the ocean
throw out an arm
let its weight fall across me

as a rope from boat to shore.

What's The Point of It?

You away with another
not your wife but good as.
What am I doing, tell me –
meeting and loving and going
and coming. What's in it?

Answer.

Do you once think of me
now where you are
living and working and loving
and talking. Eating
of course –

I am part of silence,
there in darkness.
The unknown.

Where is my shout?

Requiem For a Brother

Your brother has not left
he is around the place

he has just gone
outside for a while

he'll be back
he has a joke to tell you –

he's saying he's off
that there is somewhere to visit

but he's not leaving really,
it's not possible, you're brothers.

He's talking to your
    mother
and giving your father
    a hand
He's talking to himself
    as you do.

This is time for him
to do other things – go home

for a while, sort things out,
see the neighbours

but he'll be here.
He'll keep a sweet eye on his wife

and you will hear him laugh
now and then

when he drops in
to share secrets with you –

remind you, he's
still up to mischief.

The Kind Provider

There is no mantle that I can lay down,
no comfort I can pull from the hedgerows.

Grief looks out with his plain stare

then goes around the corner, knows
we can only take him by degrees.
Knows he is needed. That he has to come
but not at once. First shock
paralyses with his mute needle.

So on goes the body, mind, heart,
tick tock, doing, doing,
managing and ordering this and that.
Grief waits until asked,
is appalling and healthy.

Grief waters the garden in the night time.

With grief, we find a pathway.
Grief kindly provides a river